DEDICATION

I DEDICATE THIS BOOK TO MY DAUGHTER, KYLEIGH, WHO STANDS AS MY INSPIRATION FOR JUSTICE AND ACCOUNTABILITY.

Copyright ©2023 by Dontaye Carter

All rights reserved.

Published by Carter Media Group, 227 Sandy Springs Place, D368, Sandy Springs, GA 30350. Copyright ©2023 by Carter Media Group, LLC. International copyrights reserved in all countries. No portion of this book may be reproduced in any form without written permission from the publisher or author, except as permitted by U.S. copyright law.

This publication is designed to provide accurate and authoritative information in regard to the subject matter covered. It is sold with the understanding that neither the author nor the publisher is engaged in rendering legal, investment, accounting or other professional services. While the publisher and author have used their best efforts in preparing this book, they make no representations or warranties with respect to the accuracy or completeness of the contents of this book and specifically disclaim any implied warranties of merchantability or fitness for a particular purpose. No warranty may be created or extended by sales representatives or written sales materials. The advice and strategies contained herein may not be suitable for your situation. You should consult with a professional when appropriate. Neither the publisher nor the author shall be liable for any loss of profit or any other commercial damages, including but not limited to special, incidental, consequential, personal, or other damages.

Book Cover by Kevin Conwell, Sr.

Illustrations by Kevin Conwell, Sr.

979-8-9873400-0-4 edition 2023

www.mydaddyandmebook.com

Hi friends!
My name is Kyleigh.
Can I tell you about my daddy?
My daddy,
I love my daddy.

Some kids want to be firefighters, doctors, or teachers.

There are a few things that I want to be besides being like my Daddy.

My daddy tells me that he had dreams of me from the moment he met my mommy.

He says he dreams about my dreams and hopes.

I respond,

"I'm just Kyleigh."

But he says,

"You are so much more."

Why can't my daddy understand I'm only four?

But he says, "I always wanted more from the time Cupid struck me on the dance floor."

As corny as my dad was, my mommy gave him a chance, and from that moment on, they found their rhythm in life and began to dance.

I was the missing piece that made this happy house a home.

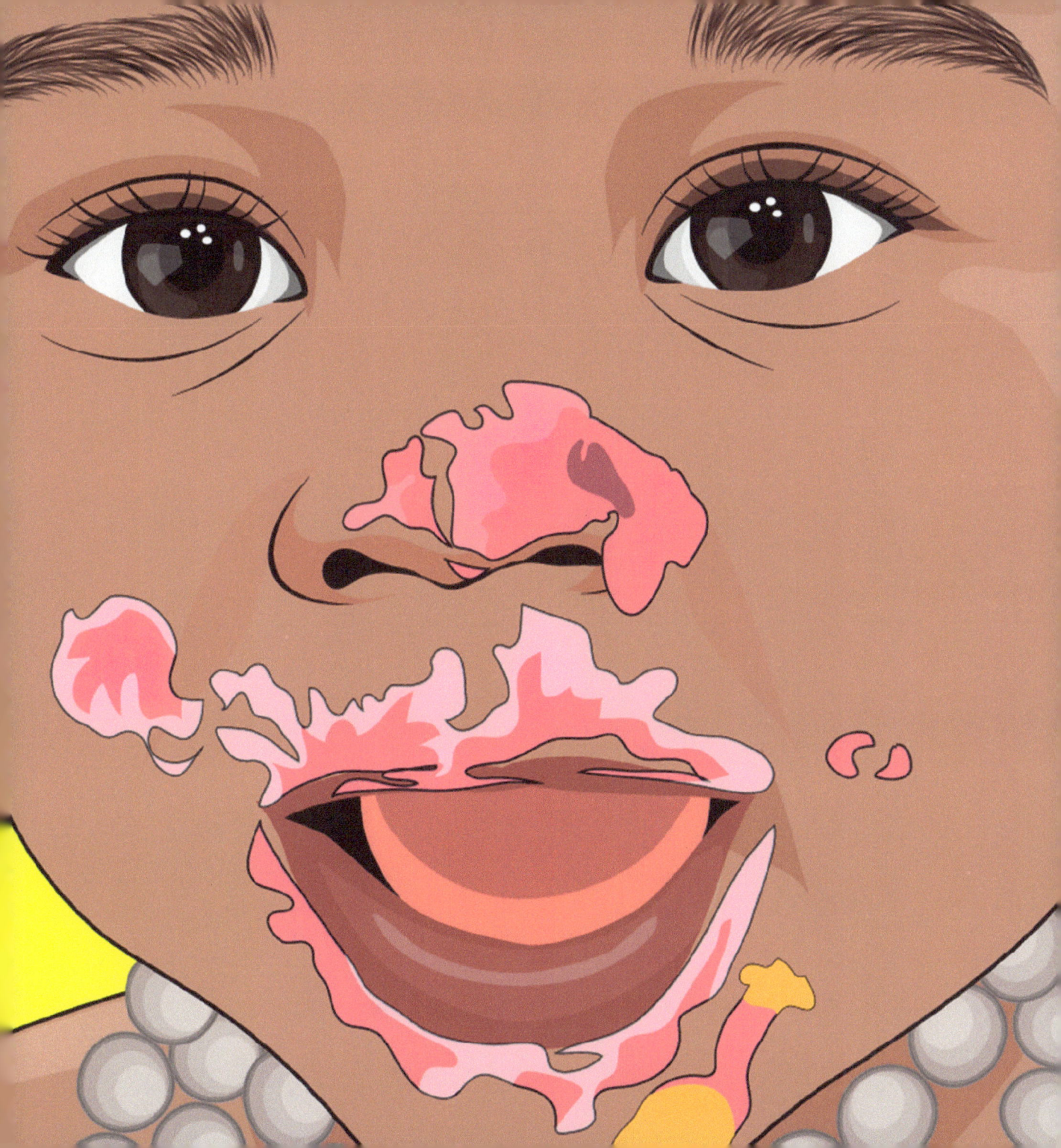

Daddy won three awards for his public relations work for attorneys fighting for social justice. He said, "You and your mommy are my reason why."

Daddy says, "I dream about the world my Kyleigh will change."

MY DADDY AND ME

Acknowledgments

Thank you to everyone who has poured into my life. I am an inspiration to many because you all wrapped your loving arms around me.

Mom, thank you for planting the seed of vision and teaching me to work towards my aspirations regardless of the obstacles.

Karen, your vision for us transformed me and the world around us. And where would I be without the guy in the sky?

Thank you, God, for your unwavering love and protection.

This book exists because of You!

Kevin Conwell Sr. is a marketing strategist with a passion for the community. He is the chairman of The Conwell Group, LLC., a modern-day consulting and communications holding company. Additionally, Kevin is the founder of both Wake Hustle Grind for Profit and Wake Hustle Grind Non-Profit. He is the CEO and lead graphic designer/creative director for 3kpmarketing.com.

Since 2007, Kevin has successfully managed a full-service advertising agency catering to Government Agencies, Non-Profit Organizations, Tech Startups, Fortune 100 companies, and Small Business Startups.

He has overseen projects totaling over $500 million throughout the United States and internationally. Kevin earned his BA in Marketing from Cleveland State University.

He actively engages in mentorship, coaching, educational teaching, training, workshops, and providing human services to youth and adults to enhance their quality of life.

Email: info@kevinconwell.com
Social Media: @Wakehustlegrind_ceo
Website: www.KevinConwell.com

www.wakehustlegrind.com

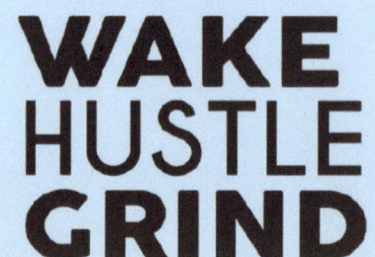

Dontaye Carter is a communication strategist and content creator passionate about storytelling. Dontaye graduated from Florida A&M University, where he studied Broadcast Journalism.

Before graduating, Dontaye worked as a video editor, Producer, and Executive Producer. He later transitioned to working on-air as a reporter.

After hanging up his microphone, Dontaye led the Publication Relations Department for the Fulton County District Attorney's office before starting his firm, Carter Media Group. Dontaye worked with the attorneys representing the victims' families in the Surviving R Kelly case. He was also one of the communication strategists hired to help raise awareness about the Ahmaud Arbery case. He began writing "My Daddy and Me" in 2022 with his daughter Kyleigh. For many of the national cases that Dontaye has worked on, Kyleigh has been by his side. This book was birthed out of Dontaye and Kyleigh's discussions about building a better world. Dontaye is passionate about mentoring, community building, and changing the narrative around Black men and fatherhood.

Email: Dontaye@Cartermedia.net
Social Media: @MyDaddyAndMeBook
Website: www.MyDaddyAndMeBook.com

www.mydaddyandmebook.com

www.ingramcontent.com/pod-product-compliance
Lightning Source LLC
Chambersburg PA
CBHW040722060526
44119CB00080B/295